DOSTOEVSKY IN 90 MINUTES

Dostoevsky
IN 90 MINUTES

Paul Strathern

IVAN R. DEE
CHICAGO

DOSTOEVSKY IN 90 MINUTES. Copyright © 2004 by Paul
Strathern. All rights reserved, including the right to reproduce
this book or portions thereof in any form. For information,
address: Ivan R. Dee, Publisher, 1332 North Halsted Street,
Chicago 60622. Manufactured in the United States of America
and printed on acid-free paper.

Library of Congress Cataloging-in-Publication Data:
Strathern, Paul, 1940–
    Dostoevsky in 90 minutes / Paul Strathern.
       p. cm.
    Includes bibliographical references and index.
    ISBN 1-56663-587-X (cloth : alk. paper) —
    ISBN 1-56663-588-8 (pbk. : alk. paper)
    1. Dostoevsky, Fyodor, 1821–1881. I. Title: Dostoevsky in
ninety minutes: II. Title.

PG3328.S77 2004
891.73'3—dc22

                                   2004048613

Contents

DOSTOEVSKY IN 90 MINUTES

Introduction

At dawn on December 22, 1849, the twenty-eight-year-old Fyodor Dostoevsky and his fellow prisoners were led out into the square of the Semyonovsky Barracks in St. Petersburg. Across the snow was a line of soldiers with rifles, facing three grey wooden posts close to the wall. The conspirators were lined up, and one by one their names were read out, followed by the words "to be put to death by firing squad." This was the first they had heard of their sentence, which came like a bolt from the blue.

The prisoners were made to kneel in the snow, and the priest read out the last rites over their heads, ". . . for the wages of sin is death."

Years later, Dostoevsky would describe his reactions, in the third person, as he waited for the sentence to be carried out: "There was a church not far off, its gilded roof glittering in the bright sun. He remembered staring with awful intensity at that roof and at the sunbeams flashing from it; he could not tear his eyes from those rays of light; they seemed to him to be his new nature and he felt that in three minutes he would somehow merge with them."

The first three prisoners were led forward and bound to the posts with ropes, their arms tied firmly behind their backs, linen hoods pulled over their heads. Dostoevsky was one of the next three in line. The officer shouted his order, and the soldiers of the firing squad raised their rifles.

The sound of galloping hooves approached. The rider and his horse clattered to a halt beside the officer and handed him a sealed packet. The officer tore open the seal and read out the message: "By the infinite clemency of His Majesty Tsar Nicholas I . . ." The prisoners' sentences of death were commuted. Dostoevsky would later write: "I cannot recall any day as happy as that one." He was lucky: one of his fellow conspirators had been driven insane by the ordeal—which had in fact been no more than a cruel charade from the outset, arranged by the tsar himself to teach Dostoevsky and his fellow prisoners a lesson they would never forget. Dostoevsky would certainly never forget the experience. He would later write: "Do you know what a death sentence means? He who has not gazed upon death cannot understand it."

Anyone who has undergone such an experience is not about to take things lightly. This would certainly be true of Dostoevsky, in both his life and his work.

Dostoevsky's Life and Works

Fyodor Mikhailovich Dostoevsky was born in Moscow in 1821 on Sunday, October 30—or November 11 according to the modern calendar. Indicatively, Russia was at the time twelve days behind Western Europe. In many other aspects, such as peasant life in the rural areas, Russia was centuries behind much of Western Europe. Life in the two main cities—St. Petersburg, the "European" capital, and Moscow, the city of "Holy Russia"—was also unsynchronized with that of Western Europe and the Atlantic seaboard of North America. Russia was still ruled by an autocratic tsar (like the German kaiser, this derives from the Latin *caesar*). He ruled by a divine right supported by the Orthodox church, which was directly descended from the eastern church of Constantinople, not Rome, and unlike Western Christendom had seen no Reformation. Likewise, Russian civilization had undergone no Renaissance. Only in the previous century had the Russian people begun to absorb certain modern European ways, largely forced on them by Peter the Great. Imported mathematicians and scientists had soon begun to thrive at court; yet the people resisted the introduction of the potato.

For all this, Russia was one of the largest and most powerful empires in the world—quite the match of the contemporary French and British empires as well as its neighbors, the Austro-Hungarian and Ottoman empires. Russian society had a heavy military emphasis—even civil servants wore uniforms denoting rank. But most of all, Russia had people and territory. The far-flung population ran into tens of millions: its exact figure was a state secret, but in a typically Russian anomaly no one really knew what it was because there was no reliable comprehensive census, only systematic guesswork. Meanwhile its territory, which occupied Finland, Poland, and the Baltic states to the west, was spreading east of the Caspian Sea into Kazakhstan toward Persia and India, and had already stretched across the Bering Straits into America, where it occupied the whole of Alaska. From east to west, the Russian Empire stretched halfway round the globe.

Dostoevsky's father Mikhail (from whom Fyodor inherited his middle name, Mikhailovich: "son of Mikhail," in the Russian tradition) was descended from a family of lapsed nobility which could trace its origins back several centuries. Mikhail Andreevich Dostoevsky had been a military surgeon but had recently retired from the army and become a doctor at the Mariinski Hospital for the Poor in Moscow. He was a man given to violent rages and deep introspective depressions. Dostoevsky's mother Maria Nechaeva was the daughter of a rich merchant who had come down in the world somewhat. According to one of Maria's many whimsical tales, her father had lost most of his fortune when he had fled Moscow before the advancing French army of Napoleon. While crossing a frozen river in his carriage, the ice had broken and his belongings had been plunged into the water, with the result that all his wads of banknotes had become so wet that they could not be separated. Maria was a cultured, gentle woman of weak health, who was both religious and extremely superstitious. These contrasting qualities of Dostoevsky's mother and father would fuse in his character to make a highly unpredictable, compulsive personality, given equally to self-destructive and confessional urges.

Young Fyodor grew up with his older brother and younger sisters within the grounds of the Mariinski Hospital, in an annex to the main building. The hospital had originally been built as the grandiose residence of a successful Italian architect, who had incorporated such features as a pediment with Doric columns. By contrast, the surrounding district was known as "The Poorhouse": one of the worst slums in Moscow, a haunt of criminals and impoverished workers, notorious for its alcoholism, murders, and disease. The inhabitants of its narrow lanes and ramshackle dwellings provided the patients for the hospital.

Dostoevsky's father discouraged visitors to their residence, and his children grew up in isolation, educated at home—tyrannized by their increasingly alcoholic father and vainly protected by their ineffectual mother, with whom young Fyodor would form a strong bond. Fyodor and his brother occasionally ventured into the hospital grounds where the wan and shaking patients wandered in their hospital gowns made of shapeless grey cloth. Around this time Fyodor caught an illness during which he lost his voice; when his voice returned it was described as having a peculiar low "artificial" tone, causing those who listened to him to feel strangely uncomfortable—a socially upsetting trait that he would retain throughout his life. There was little refreshing normality in the Dostoevsky household, and as one of Fyodor's later characters would exclaim: "We are all unaccustomed to life."

In 1827 Dostoevsky's father was promoted to a civil service rank that entitled him to the privileges of the gentry. As a result, four years later he was able to buy an estate at Darovoe, deep in the countryside of the Tula region, 150 versts (100 miles) south of Moscow. The grounds of the estate were roughly eight miles long by three miles wide, and contained two villages comprising "one hundred souls." These were the serfs, who were literally owned by the estate. (Britain would abolish slavery two years later; Russia would not abolish its serfdom until 1861—four years before the United States passed the Thirteenth Amendment abolishing slavery after the Civil War). The Darovoe estate was badly run-down. It had no rivers or woods and consisted largely of scrubland and poor soil, riven by the occasional gulley. The serfs were ground down by poverty and lived in huts with thatched roofs (which in lean years were pulled off to feed the livestock.) The main residence was simply a mud-brick manor house with a thatched roof. Even during the long summer holidays that the Dostoevskys spent here, family life was as gloomy and isolated as ever.

At the age of thirteen Fyodor joined his older brother at a private school in Moscow, and at sixteen he was sent to the Academy of Military Engineering in St. Petersburg. By now his mother had become so weak and ill that she was confined to bed in a darkened room, where she died in 1837.

Fyodor's mother had always encouraged him to read, and now he lost himself in books, even beginning a novel of his own set in Vienna. By this time his father had retired from the Mariinski Hospital and lived permanently on the estate at Darovoe. Here he sank into alcoholism and degeneracy. During his fits of rage he would flog the serfs mercilessly, and took to debauching their young daughters. The serfs were eventually driven beyond endurance. One summer morning when he set out from Darovoe in his carriage, a group of serfs waylaid him on a deserted country track, crushed his testicles with their bare hands, and forced his vodka down his throat until he choked to death. When news of this reached Fyodor in St. Petersburg, he suffered such an overload of contradictory feelings that he fell to the floor in convulsions, and then fainted. This is generally accepted as the first manifestation of the epilepsy that would plague Dostoevsky throughout the rest of his life.

During his last years at the military academy, Dostoevsky continued to read avidly, devouring the great European classics such as Homer, Shakespeare, and Schiller. He also developed a taste for gothic horror stories, and this interest in sensational material would have a formative effect. But most of all he was spellbound by the contemporary Russian writer Gogol, who had only recently sprung to fame with his tragicomic stories. These were among the first realistic depictions of Russian life, holding up a mirror to the society of the time. Their mixture of realism and satire sprang from a romantic temperament driven to distraction by the crassness and evil of the corrupt world in which he found himself. Dostoevsky deeply empathized with this writer who could neither accept the world nor successfully isolate himself from its pains. 1842 saw the publication of Gogol's masterpiece *Dead Souls*, which faithfully depicts the serfdom and bureaucratic corruption of a land, large regions of which remained feudal. Readers soon appreciated the true picture that lay behind the satire; Dostoevsky took the book to heart.

In 1843 Dostoevsky graduated from the military academy, and after completing his compulsory year of military service he resigned his commission to become a writer. This was a brave decision, renouncing financial security for the vagaries of bohemian life in St. Petersburg, where during a cold winter penniless intellectuals were liable to freeze to death in their attic rooms. But Dostoevsky's period of obscurity did not last long. In 1846 he published his first novel, *Poor Folk*, which was quickly recognized by the critics and became something of an overnight success.

Poor Folk is a curious work, with many anomalies. For a start, it takes the form of an exchange of letters, an early novelistic form which had long gone out of fashion. Likewise, its central theme was hardly original. A poor but worthy forty-seven-year-old copying clerk, Makar Devushkin, whose home is the dirty corner of a kitchen, exchanges letters with the seventeen-year-old Varvara Dobroselova, who in many ways is more worldly-wise. Much of this novel clearly resembles Gogol's story "The Overcoat," which is also about a copying clerk.

But Dostoevsky's work is shot through with an entirely original psychological understanding. Unlike Gogol's comic hero, Devushkin is deeply self-aware and experiences painful humiliations. Beset by poverty, Varvara is procured for an unfeeling rich man. Later she resists his further advances until eventually he proposes to her. She accepts, and Devushkin is crushed. Apart from the many insights of character that Dostoevsky manages to imply through the epistolary form, the novel also contains an atmospheric evocation of St. Petersburg, much of which was then less than fifty years old.

The merit of *Poor Folk* was recognized by the leading literary critic Vissarion Belinsky. He welcomed Dostoevsky into his circle, which included such glittering literary figures as Nekrasov and Turgenev. But Dostoevsky found himself ill at ease among such luminaries. He was both touchy and shy: his voice and manner made those who met him ill at ease, and it was evident to many that he despised them. Belinsky had seen in *Poor Folk* a deep concern for the plight of the poor, which was in accord with his own reformist views. Yet while Dostoevsky certainly sympathized with the poor, his deeper concern was with the spiritual and psychological aspects of his characters. This became evident in his next important work, a novella called *The Double*. Here we enter into the nightmare world of a middle-ranking civil servant called Golyadkin, whose mind appears to be disintegrating. During the course of the novella he encounters his "double," who appears at one stage to be no more than his reflection in a glass, at another to be a distinct human being who shares his name and appearance, at other moments a "split" aspect of Golyadkin's character who berates him for his morbid sensitivity. Here we experience many of the classic signs of schizophrenia, though at the time such pathological symptoms were neither recognized nor understood. As such, this is a pioneer work. We accompany Golyadkin on his way as he upsets, and is upset by, the various people he encounters, including his disconcerted doctor, the guests at an excruciating dinner party, and his disapproving servant Petrushka ("Respectable people don't have doubles").

Dostoevsky considered *The Double* to be "ten times superior" to *Poor Folk*, and he was deeply upset when it was rejected by the critics. In fact this was not surprising. *The Double* is an awkward work, in many ways as tiresome as its "hero," who ends up being led away to the insane asylum. "Our hero shrieked and clutched at his head. Alas! This was what he had known for a long time would happen!" It is difficult to retain sympathy for the often bewildering and pretentious Golyadkin. Only the deep psychological insight into mental disturbance shown by the author is exceptional, indicative of his great works to come. Dostoevsky was feeling his way blindly toward what he wanted to say, but he did not yet fully know what he wanted to describe or how to describe it. He was merely trying to follow his own instincts—an ambitious attempt which in this case resulted in failure, shot through with elements of clumsy brilliance and originality. No one had ever described a mind like this before.

Belinsky was disappointed, and already Turgenev had collaborated in a poem which satirized Dostoevsky as "The Knight of the Doleful

Countenance"—a reference to his appearance as well as his resemblance to a ludicrous Quixote figure. (Dostoevsky never forgave or forgot this, and twenty-five years later he would include a coruscating caricature of Turgenev in his novel *The Possessed*.) Dostoevsky took his company elsewhere and began frequenting the more radical Petrashevsky Circle, a group of intellectuals who were attracted to the idea of a socialist utopia. They believed that only with the establishment of such a society could the full potential of human nature be realized. The activities of the group consisted largely of discussions, and their aims were political, though once again Dostoevsky's participation in the group was misunderstood. His interests lay more in the potentialities of the human spirit than in the society where this might be achieved. Despite this, Dostoevsky became involved in a more revolutionary faction within the group. This had its own printing press and believed in circulating propaganda leaflets.

For almost a quarter-century Russia had been languishing under the rule of the tyrannical Tsar Nicholas I, who would countenance no change whatsoever throughout the land. In pursuance of this policy, his secret political police were ordered to bring in "reports about all occurrences without exception." The Petrashevsky Circle was penetrated by a police informer who reported on their activities. His report on Dostoevsky described him as "giving the impression of being a real conspirator: he was taciturn, liked to talk confidentially to people, he was secretive rather than outspoken."

At 4 a.m. on April 29, 1849, the police raided Dostoevsky's rented apartment and arrested him. Other members of the Petrashevsky Circle were also rounded up. They were all confined in the forbidding Peter and Paul Fortress, overlooking the River Neva in the center of the city. Symbolically, this had been the first major building erected in St. Petersburg, and the laying of its foundation stone by Peter the Great in 1703 is taken as the founding date of the city. Many leading figures in Russian history would be imprisoned here—from the Decembrists (the military officers who had rebelled en masse in 1825), to the anarchist Bakunin, through to Lenin himself (after whom the city would later be named for more than seventy years). Dostoevsky was held in a solitary cell, emerging only for interrogation. This was conducted by a military tribunal headed by the fortress's aged governor, General Nabokov, who had fought Napoleon at the Battle of Borodino. His great-grandnephew, who would become a writer in the following century, would claim that when the general learned that Dostoevsky was a writer, he loaned him books from his private collection to read in his cell. This fond fantasy is not borne out by the transcript of Dostoevsky's interrogation:

Dostoevsky: I am not guilty.
Nabokov: You are caught out by your own lies. . . . Read this. [He hands Dostoevsky a note circulated amongst the Petrashevsky Circle, which states: "The time has come for insurrection . . . having armed myself, I undertake to participate fully."]
Dostoevsky: I never signed this.

> *Nabokov*: You must tell this secret tribunal every single thing you know. . . . If you lie or are obstinate, do you know what will happen?
> *Dostoevsky*: No, I do not.
> *Nabokov*: . . . the penalty for conspiracy against the government is shameful death by hanging, or being quartered [body hacked into four pieces, or pulled apart by four horses].

This does not sound like the tone that would be adopted by the prisoner's thoughtful librarian.

Dostoevsky and his fellow conspirators were detained in solitary confinement for eight months. Not surprisingly, the hypersensitive Dostoevsky began suffering from all manner of ailments, a condition which was hardly helped by his lifelong hypochondria. In a letter, he tells his brother:

> My hemorrhoids are driving me to desperation and I have a pain in my chest which I have never had before . . . my supersensitiveness becomes morbidly alert, especially toward evening; at night I have long, hideous dreams. Moreover, for some time now I can-

not get rid of the impression that the floor is rocking under me and, sitting in my cell, I feel as though I were in a cabin on board ship. All this leads me to the conclusion that my nerves are getting more and more frayed. . . . I have to restrain myself for fear of a breakdown.

And so on. The man who had so powerfully imagined the mental disintegration of *The Double* was now on the verge of entering its reality. Then, one morning, without warning and with no idea of what was happening to them, Dostoevsky and his fellow conspirators were transported to the Semyonovsky Square for the hideous farce of their mock execution.

This experience would have a lasting effect on Dostoevsky, and he would return to it again and again in his writing. Although always a spiritually intense young man, he had by this stage developed a skeptical attitude toward religion, along with a materialistic view of life which was shared by many Russian intellectuals of the period. But from now on all this would change. He would come to see life as a sacred gift. Where previously he had been idealistic, he would now aspire to an uncompromising spiritual integrity. Instead of the mock execution cowing him, or breaking him (as it had some of the others), if anything it intensified his awareness of his own individual responsibility for all that he did.

Afterward Dostoevsky was sentenced to four years hard labor, followed by service as an army private in Siberia for an unspecified period. The prisoners were taken away to the blacksmith, where their ankles were fettered in irons weighing ten pounds. They were then bundled, hobbling, into horse-drawn sledges between armed guards and set off on the sixteen-day journey through the snow for Siberia. As they left Europe, crossing the Ural Mountains almost a thousand miles from St. Petersburg, the temperature dropped to minus forty degrees Fahrenheit, and the horses began stumbling through snowdrifts.

From the age of twenty-eight until he was thirty-two, Dostoevsky endured the horrific barbarities of the penal colony at Tobolsk. The miserable unsustaining diet of watery cabbage soup with cockroaches; the filth and vermin and noise of the barracks (even when a man moved in the night his chains rattled); the sadism of the guards and the brutalizing regime; working as a laborer even when the mercury froze in the thermometer; the contempt of the peasant and serf convicts for the "gentry" prisoners ("You used to torment the people; now that you are the worst of the worst, you want to be our brothers")—all this would be vividly evoked in the book that Dostoevsky later wrote of his experiences, the aptly named *House of the Dead*. This is cast as a novel. The main story is told in the first person by the landowner Goryanchikov, who had murdered his wife in a fit of jealousy and been sentenced to ten years hard labor. The grueling misery of the regime had ground down Goryanchikov, breaking his spirit, so that after his release into exile he had become "a terrible misanthrope, who kept apart from all society." The author describes meeting Goryanchikov in the small Siberian town where he is living out his exile. After Goryanchikov dies, the author discovers at his poor lodgings some papers with an "incoherent and fragmentary" narrative, interspersed with "terrible recollections thrown in convulsively as if torn from the author."

This aptly sets the tone of the pitiful story to come, with its succession of horrors. . . . The ritual of going through "Green Street" (two rows of soldiers armed with green rods, between which prisoners sentenced to corporal punishment had to pass). The drunken major in charge of the prisoners who was "severe to the point of insanity." Glimpses of the Kirghiz tribespeople who lived on the steppes outside the prison: "wild, savage, poverty-stricken; but they were free." And of course the many, vividly described convicts. It is these inhabitants of the "Dead-House," and their barely human life, which make this work so riveting. Here is Dostoevsky's first cast of raw, utterly degraded characters, mere fragments of human portraits, whose pigments will become such an integral part of his palette. Yet these exaggerated characters were not quite what they seemed. Although the narrator Goryanchikov was a fiction, it is now known that the descriptions of his fellow prisoners were precise portraits which remained true to life.

Here was a humanity exaggerated by the conditions under which it was forced to live. Even at his most extreme, Dostoevsky would usually remain uncannily close to life.

Yet he would also seek to understand that life. Few of the characters in *House of the Dead* have any redeeming features, and none are redeemed by their prison experience. Dostoevsky himself, on the other hand, survived his ordeal with some remnant of his spirit intact. He would suffer lasting physical and psychological scars, yet at the same time he would retain the conviction that somehow the core of his being had been revealed to him. He found faith in himself, and the strength to cling to his self-belief. He also found God—and a deep-rooted but nonetheless troubled religious faith that would last throughout his life. He attempted to express this ineffable yet contradictory experience: "I am a child of this age, a child of unbelief and doubts, even to this very day, and shall remain so (I know this) until the day I am laid in my coffin." Still, he could lay claim to having discovered his lasting credo "where everything is clear and sacred for me . . . to believe that nothing is more beautiful, profound, sympathetic, reasonable, manly and more perfect than Christ." This was no ordinary belief, more a recipe for constant spiritual turmoil which seemed to match the requirements of his peculiar psychology.

In 1854 Dostoevsky was released from prison and drafted into the army as a private in the pioneer town of Semipalatinsk, at the frontier of Kazakhstan (nearly two thousand miles from St. Petersburg). Life in the army in the Wild East of Russia was hardly comfortable, but at least it meant freedom. After two years Dostoevsky was promoted to lieutenant. It was during this period that he met and fell in love with Maria Dimitriyevna Isayeva, the wife of a former teacher reduced to becoming a customs officer, who was far gone in alcoholism. When her husband died, Dostoevsky married her. Maria was in her thirties, blonde, and with a dependent son. Together with Dostoevsky she shared a fierce belief in justice, and like him was emotionally intense. She also shared her new husband's emotional instability, was prone to hysteria, and suffered from deteriorating tuberculosis. On their brief honeymoon, Dostoevsky had one of his increasingly frequent fits of epilepsy—hardly an auspicious start to a marriage which Dostoevsky appears to have entered into in desperation, his longing for a partner having become all but unbearable for him. On the other hand, Maria's emotions appear to have been closer to resignation, there being no other way for her to obtain emotional and financial support.

By now the autocratic reign of Tsar Nicholas I had given way to the more liberal government of Alexander II. Dostoevsky was permitted to move to Tver, just a hundred miles from Moscow, and finally in 1860 was allowed to move back to St. Petersburg. Here, after an absence of more than ten years, he set about trying to establish himself once again as a writer. Together with his brother Mikhail, he set up a magazine called *Vremya* (Time). Dostoevsky now began writing *House of the Dead*, which appeared episode by episode in the magazine until it was closed down by the authorities in 1863.

A year later *House of the Dead* was published in its entirety. This marked the beginning of a

Russian literary tradition—the prison novel—which would continue until the late twentieth century and the works of Alexander Solzhenitsyn. This grim genre would produce many inspiring testaments to the human spirit, though few would match the literary power of Dostoevsky's pioneer work. 1864 also saw the opening of another magazine by Dostoevsky and his brother, called *Epokha* (Epoch), which soon began featuring episodes from a new book by Dostoevsky called *Notes from the Underground*.

This opens with the lines: "I am a sick man. I am full of spleen and repellent. I believe I am diseased, but I know nothing whatsoever about my disease. I do not know for certain what ails me." Although there are echoes of *The Double* here, *Notes from the Underground* in fact introduces an entirely new kind of human being to literature. This is not an attempt to portray a character suffering from mental illness but "a representative figure from a generation still surviving," as Dostoevsky himself put it. "This personage introduces himself and his outlook on life, and tries, as it were, to elucidate the causes that brought about, inevitably brought about, his appearance in our midst." But the unnamed narrator does not succeed in explaining himself away as a mere passing social phenomenon. Instead he reveals the innermost depths of his being:

> In order to act, one must be absolutely sure of oneself, no doubts must remain anywhere. But how am I, for example, to be sure of myself? Where are the primary causes on which I can take my stand, where are my foundations? Where am I to take them from? I practice thinking, and consequently each of my primary causes pulls along another, even more primary, in its wake, and so on *ad infinitum.*

His very humanity appears to him as a sickness. He is filled with angst and anger, beset by an overwhelming sense of alienation, but can find no reason to explain this. Here Dostoevsky is at his most prophetic. Such feelings would soon begin to spread like a contagion through a certain class of disaffected young European intellectuals. To them it seemed that their life—indeed life itself—had somehow become utterly futile.

Notes from the Undergound is a work of such penetrating psychological acumen that it remains to this day a masterpiece of self-discovery. Yet amidst all its flailings of inner exploration it reaches no firm conclusion. Humanity was in the process of transformation: there could be no fixed object of self-knowledge. Adrift in the verbal flow of one's consciousness, one could only attempt to express the drift of one's bewilderment. The narrator of *Notes from the Underground* is a forty-year-old former civil servant living in St. Petersburg in a single room. All he can do is think his thoughts, constantly racked by the impossibleness of his existence and his "complicated state of mind." He is filled with an existential unease and spleen, yet "even in the moment of acutest spleen, I was inwardly conscious with shame that I was not only not spiteful but not even an embittered man, that I was simply scaring sparrows at random and amusing myself by it." His spleen is in a way a diversion, an act—not to disguise himself, but simply because he does not know what to do with himself. There is no longer any correct way to be, to act.

All values are relative, and there is no absolute truth. (In just a few years' time, in Western Europe, Nietzsche would loudly proclaim what Hegel had already quietly noted: "God is dead.")

The Underground Man feels himself to be dislocated from the everyday world going on around him. This makes him feel that he is somehow not himself; yet he has no real idea of how to be himself. He doesn't know how to be *anything*. At one point he poignantly declares that he "could not even become an insect." He is aware of his place in the scientific scheme of things, but this only further exasperates him. "My anger, in consequence of the damned laws of consciousness, is subject to chemical decomposition. As you look, its object vanishes into thin air, its reason evaporates, the offender is nowhere to be found, the affront ceases to be an affront and becomes destiny, something like a toothache, for which no one is responsible." As an object of science, human life has become wholly determined, its every act a link in the inexorable chain of cause and effect. He feels stifled by rational humanism and progress. "Civilization develops in man nothing but an added capacity to receive impressions—that is all." He feels a great hunger for some new form of spirituality.

The first thirty-page section of this "short fiction" is heavy going, concentrated in its concentration upon self, yet it remains one of the finest passages of sustained introspection in Western literature. It is at the same time literature, psychology, and philosophy—but devoid of message, of comforting answer. *Notes from the Underground* is also utterly modern. Who, in all honesty, can say that he or she has not experienced such feelings, such angst? They are that part of our humanity which lies beneath the surface of our contemporary life.

In 1864 Dostoevsky suffered a double blow when the two people closest to him both died. His wife Maria finally succumbed to tuberculosis in April, and three months later his beloved brother Mikhail died. Dostoevsky quixotically vowed to support his wife's wastrel son and his brother's family, a gesture he could ill afford when *Epokha* collapsed, leaving a large printing debt which he could not pay. He was now in his early forties, counting himself alone in the world, but once more with a growing literary reputation. Desperately he set about trying to find another wife. His alternately earnest and unstable emotional state handicapped his attempts to woo a rich woman writer, and she turned him down almost as soon as his intentions became clear. He then embarked upon an affair with another woman writer, twenty years younger than himself, Apollinaria Suslova, whom he had met when she began contributing her work to *Vremya*. To avoid his creditors and seek relief from his epilepsy, Dostoevsky and his new lover embarked upon a trip to Western Europe, traveling through Italy, France, and Germany. This became ever more emotionally fraught as Apollinaria alternated between loving him and despising him, a regime which appears to have suited the masochistic elements in Dostoevsky's character but did little for his mental stability. He developed a mania for gambling, frantically losing at the casinos what little money was sent to him by his Russian publishers and all he could borrow from Apollinaria.

Upon his return to Russia, Dostoevsky rashly signed a contract for a novel with an unscrupulous publisher who aimed to obtain copyright on Dostoevsky's earlier novels when the author defaulted on his tight deadline. But Dostoevsky hired a stenographer and at amazing speed dictated his short novel *The Gambler*, which describes in detail the euphoria and humiliation of succumbing to gambling addiction. Although the speed at which this work was composed may detract from its overall literary merits, its psychological veracity and intensity are undeniable. Typical is the following occasion, when the hero has won four or five times in the course of his first five minutes at the roulette table:

> I ought to have left at that point, but a strange sort of feeling came over me, a kind of desire to challenge fate, a longing to give it a fillip on the nose or stick out my tongue at it. I staked the permitted maximum—4,000 gulden—and lost. Then, getting excited, I pulled out all I had left, staked it in the same way, lost again, and after that I left the table

as if I had been stunned. I could not even grasp what had happened to me. . . . I . . . spent the time until [dinner] wandering unsteadily about in the park.

Alongside such episodes, *The Gambler* contains some superbly drawn characters, especially the thinly disguised "Polina," a striking and dominant woman who would be the first of many such women in his novels. The book also includes humor, not all of it unintentional. Dostoevsky had developed a rare ability to combine immoderate emotion with an element of levity, a gift he also retained in life. According to those who met him, he could at the same time be both a passionate and a witty companion. Dostoevsky knew himself very deeply, if often powerlessly, and this ongoing vein of humor reflects his ironic self-knowledge.

The Gambler was finished in the nick of time, largely through the assistance provided by his stenographer Anna Grigoryevna Snitkina. Dostoevsky then made a rare wise decision in his personal life: he married Anna. She was to prove his salvation. Immediately she took steps to put his finances in order, and set about establishing a stable atmosphere in which he would work. And work he did. Astonishingly, at the same time Dostoevsky had been writing *The Gambler*, he had begun working on a longer, far more ambitious novel. This made use of all the talents that had been developed for the most part separately in his previous works, combining them to produce his first transcendent masterpiece: *Crime and Punishment*.

Dostoevsky himself described this work as "a psychological account of a crime," which also had the polemical aim of exposing the "strange half-baked ideas that are floating about in the air." Despite such unpromising labels, what he actually wrote was an intense and thrilling five-hundred-page epic. Like *Notes from the Underground*, it was in many ways also a philosophical exploration. And as in *House of the Dead*, we are introduced to a world of characters driven by the extremity of their circumstances. These combine in a plot of classic simplicity. The impoverished student Raskolnikov murders the pawnbroker

Alyona Ivanova, is suspected of the crime by the detective Porfiry Petrovich, eventually confesses, and is sent to Siberia. From the start we are plunged into the atmosphere of nineteenth-century St. Petersburg during the early evening of a July heat wave. "It was terribly hot, moreover it was close, crowded; lime, scaffolding, bricks, dust everywhere, and that special summer stench known so well to every Petersburger who cannot afford to rent a summer house." We join Raskolnikov, who is "remarkably good-looking, taller than average, slender and trim, with beautiful dark eyes and dark blond hair," as he passes among the slum streets of taverns and tenements, "muttering to himself from time to time in his habitual monologue." As he says of himself, "I babble too much . . . That's why I don't do anything, because I babble."

As we are introduced into the atmosphere of Raskolnikov's mind, we become aware how "the loathsome and melancholy coloring of the picture" around him is affecting "the young man's already overwrought nerves." Dostoevsky originally intended to write this novel in the first person, as if told by Raskolnikov. Instead it is narrated in the more traditional third person—yet there is no omniscient narrator. For the most part, what we see, hear, and feel is Raskolnikov: his feelings, perceptions, and thoughts. We are drawn into his world, experiencing his surroundings through his distorting vision. We are afraid with him, we live his plight. His nerve-induced sensitivity is apparent from the moment he emerges from his room, "located just under the floor of a tall, five-storied house . . . more like a cupboard than a room." On the floor below he sneaks past the open door to the kitchen of his landlady, to whom he owes back rent. As he does so he feels a "painful and cowardly sensation, which made him wince with shame." But he is also proud, feeling himself to be somehow superior to all this. He claims he is not afraid of his landlady, "whatever she might be plotting against him"; yet he still tells himself, "better to steal catlike down the stairs somehow and slip away unseen." Raskolnikov is a complex and contradictory character, but these very contradictions make him so real.

As he walks along the street, the drunken driver of a large horse and cart shouts down at him, mocking him on account of his tall, cylindrical German hat. This is unmistakably a product of smart Nevsky Prospect but now "all worn out, quite faded, all holes and stains, brimless, and dented." Under his breath Raskolnikov berates himself for drawing attention to himself, the last thing he wishes to do, as he makes his way to "the enormous house beside the canal," the tenement where the pawnbroker Alyona Ivanova lives on the fourth floor. He rings her bell, and "the door was opened a tiny crack. [She looked] at the visitor through the crack with obvious mistrust, and only her little eyes could be seen glittering from the darkness." When she opens the door we see "a tiny dried-up old crone, about sixty, with sharp, spiteful little eyes and a small, sharp nose. Her long, thin neck, which resembled a chicken's leg, was wrapped in some flannel rags and, despite the heat, a fur-trimmed jacket, completely worn out and yellow with age." To her too he owes money.

This is the woman he plans to murder, and later—by now inescapably immersed in Raskolnikov's thoughts and feelings—we follow him as he goes about the "crime" of the title. . . . As the old woman approaches him, complaining about the further item he wants to pawn, "he took the axe all the way out [from under his jacket], swung it with both hands, scarcely aware of himself, and almost without effort, almost mechanically, brought the butt-end down on her head. His own strength seemed to have no part in it. But the moment he brought the axe down, strength was born in him."

He takes the old woman's keys. "He was in full possession of his reason, the clouding and dizziness had ceased, but his hands were still trembling." In the bedroom he finds the old woman's trunk of pawned valuables beneath the bed. But in the midst of his search he is disturbed by a "slight but distinct cry" from the main room. Lizaveta, the old woman's downtrodden sister, is "standing in the middle of the room, with a big bundle in her hands, frozen, staring at her murdered sister, white as a sheet, and as if unable to utter a cry." When she sees Raskolnikov run into the room, she backs away from him, "staring at him fixedly, point-blank, but still not uttering a sound." As he rushes at her with the axe, "she twisted her lips pitifully, as very small children do when they begin to be afraid of something." When Raskolnikov raises the axe above her upturned face, "she brought her free left hand up, very slightly, nowhere near her face, and slowly stretched it out toward him as if to keep him away." But by now it is too late. "The blow landed directly on the skull, with the sharp edge, and immediately split the whole upper part of the forehead, almost to the crown." Raskolnikov is gripped with increasing fear "after this second, quite unexpected murder."

Such is the compelling atmosphere of the novel. But this is only part of the story. An equally gripping drama unfolds in Raskolnikov's mind as we live through the feelings of guilt, terror, and bravado that accompany his thoughts. It gradually becomes clear that Raskolnikov's major mistake has been to misjudge himself. He is an intellectual, his mind filled with the latest ideas, but he does not know himself. Here we see how a human being can be filled with ideas about the world and our place in it yet remain fatally unaware of what it means to be a human being.

Raskolnikov justifies his crime to himself rationally on various counts. One of his "principled" arguments is the utilitarian ideal, which in Dostoevsky's day had gained such support among St. Petersburg's fashionable intellectuals. According to utilitarianism, there is no such thing as an absolute morality—there is no ultimate good and evil. Instead, morality is purely a social construct. What is good is what brings the greatest amount of pleasure to the greatest number of people. By killing the despicable old woman Alyona Ivanova, Raskolnikov reasons that he is ridding the world of someone who causes misery. By taking her valuables and distributing such wealth charitably, he is also bringing pleasure to a number of people. Raskolnikov is far from an evil person through and through. In many ways he is a charitable, sympathetic human being—it is his "half-baked" ideas that open up the flaws in his character. With his new-found wealth, Raskolnikov aids the family of the alcoholic Marmeladov (based upon the former husband of Dostoevsky's wife Maria, the customs officer in Semipalatinsk who died of alcoholism). Marmeladov has been killed in an accident, and Raskolnikov gains the admiration of Marmeladov's daughter Sonya, who has been reduced to becoming a prostitute. Raskolnikov also aids his widowed mother and his valiant sister Dunya, who has become a governess and is preyed upon by her master, the evil Svidrigaylov.

Raskolnikov persuades himself that if there is no such thing as good and evil, then there is no such thing as crime. But this is not enough. Indicatively, he also feels the need to justify the murder to himself with a further argument. This other argument in fact contradicts the utilitarian argument. Raskolnikov reasons that he must assert himself as a superior being. He must impose his rational self on the undermining promptings of his unconscious mind. Following in the footsteps of great men such as Caesar and Napoleon, he has a "right to transgress" the dictates of normal morality (whose very existence he had previously denied). Morality is for ordinary people. If the great men of history had not disregarded morality, there would have been no progress. The Caesars of this world have a duty to act as they see fit. Morality is meant for the rest of humanity, who are there only to ensure the propagation of the species.

Here Dostoevsky gives voice to ideas that would receive their most articulate advocacy some decades later in the works of the German philosopher Nietzsche, with his advocacy of the "will to power" and the "superman." Many of Europe's most influential artists and writers would become advocates of Nietzsche's ideas. Shaw, Yeats, Mann, d'Annunzio, and many lesser intellectuals would all fall under the spell of such "aristocratic" ideals. But Dostoevsky also pinpointed a more covert assumption of superiority among the prevailing intellectual ideas that so appealed to Raskolnikov. A century earlier, the French romantic philosopher Rousseau had urged humanity to free itself from the chains imposed upon it by an unjust society. And those who did not voluntarily liberate themselves should be "compelled to be free." It was the duty of the intellectuals to force the downtrodden people to take possession of their liberty. Dostoevsky's warning about such views proved particularly prophetic for Russia. This would be precisely the argument used under communism to ensure conformity among the population to the regime that sought to "liberate" them.

If Raskolnikov's decision to commit murder was "rational," he could expect his subsequent behavior to be similarly rational. But this was of course not the case. His "rational" mind was submerged as his unconscious feelings welled to the surface. Yet still he attempted to cling to reason. As Raskolnikov experiences the psychological aftermath of his crime, he attempts to reason out his true motive for the murder. He finds that there appears to be no single answer. There was no defining moment when he decided to commit the crime. His mind had become made up in the course of a long series of small decisions. One thing seemed to have led to another as his mind, in the grip of some obscure obsession, moved in a dream toward committing the actual deed. Dostoevsky exhibits exceptional psychological skill and acumen in showing how Raskolnikov came to commit murder. We recognize that even the most vital decisions in our lives can be far from clear-cut. Psychology, beliefs (whether genuine or deluded), the everyday happenings that occupy our lives—all these play their cumulative part.

Similarly, we witness the workings of Raskolnikov's mind as he comes to terms with his confused feelings after having committed the murder. He understands that just as he was driven to commit the crime, he is now driven by an impulse to confess to it, or somehow to ensure that he is caught and accused of it. He feels that unless he confesses, or is arrested, his is liable to commit suicide. This awareness is borne upon Raskolnikov as he passes through a world of vivid characters, each encounter having its own illuminating effect. We meet the pompous and successful bourgeois Luzhin, with his ridiculous lorgnette and oversized gold ring, who wants to marry Raskolnikov's sister Dunya, yet treats her and her mother with disgraceful meanness. Then there is the truly evil landowner Svindrigaylov, whose outrageous behavior toward his serfs and their daughters echoes that of Dostoevsky's father. Most telling of all for Raskolnikov is his increasing involvement with Sonya, the prostitute, whom Dostoevsky depicts as a Christian figure. Her self-sacrificing love for Raskolnikov will in the end facilitate his redemption. But Raskolnikov must first be led through the maze of his fears and worries to his eventual confession of the crime and his subsequent sentence to penal servitude in Siberia. The devoted Sonya follows him, and her presence assists him in his spiritual resurrection. At one point Raskolnikov falls ill and is hospitalized. Here he has a curious nightmare, which Dostoevsky describes in some detail:

> He dreamt in his illness that the whole world was condemned to fall victim to a terrible, unknown pestilence which was moving on Europe out of the depths of Asia. All were destined to perish, except for a chosen few, a very few. There had appeared a new strain of

trichinae, microscopic creatures parasitic in men's bodies. But these creatures were endowed with intelligence and will. People who were infected immediately became like men possessed and out of their minds. But never, never, had any men thought themselves so wise and so unshakable in the truth as those who were attacked. Never had they considered their judgments, their scientific deductions, or their moral convictions and creeds more infallible.

This is Dostoevsky's antithesis of the Christian life, a form of unshakable individualism. (Here too, Dostoevsky proves uncannily prophetic: the effects of this individualistic epidemic are easily recognizable in modern scientific humanity. Indeed, to a certain extent everyone in the modern Western world has this disease—though it is only extremists and religious fundamentalists who wish to destroy this world who now regard it as a disease.)

Raskolnikov is eventually purified by his suffering, and emerges from his mental confusion to a quiet acceptance of his fate. We learn that he is on his way to redemption—presumably to become one of the "chosen few" who will survive the epidemic of individualism.

Fortunately this polemic ending does not undercut the sheer psychological power of Dostoevsky's imagination, which has driven the novel all the way to this conclusion. In an ironic echo of Raskolnikov, the profound artist in Dostoevsky was so much more powerful than his ideas. No matter his woeful forebodings with regard to the "yellow peril" of individualism, in Raskolnikov he had created one of the most profound and tragic individuals in nineteenth-century Western literature: a Hamlet for his time.

In 1867 Dostoevsky, accompanied by his new wife Anna, departed Russia for an extended stay in Europe. By July he was in Baden-Baden, the fashionable spa town in Germany. In an effort to extend his meager financial resources, Dostoevsky took to gambling again. Within days he was once more in the grip of his feverish obsession. His wife Anna described how when he was playing at the tables he "looked terrible, just as though he was drunk: his face was red and his eyes bloodshot."

At Baden-Baden, Dostoevsky called on his erstwhile friend from the Belinsky Circle, the novelist Turgenev. He was immediately put off by Turgenev's aristocratic ways, his professed atheism, and his delight at living permanently in Europe. Turgenev told him: "I consider myself to be a German and not a Russian and am proud of it." Dostoevsky was a fervent patriot, an adherent of the Slavophile—as distinct from the Europeanizing—Russian school. Turgenev wished Russia to become modern, to take on "civilized" Western ways; Dostoevsky now believed in ancient "Holy Russia" and the timeless spiritual qualities that he was convinced it possessed more than any other European country. Since the eighteenth century, Russia had been riven by this division, which was, and remains, noticeable in its arts, its politics, indeed throughout its society. In music we see this in the division between Dostoevsky's contemporaries, the "European" Tchaikovsky and the Slavophile Borodin. In the early decades of the twentieth century, after the Russian Revolution, it would surface in the advocates of "communism in one country" (led by Stalin) and their adversaries who advocated "world revolution" (led by Trotsky). Peter the Great had founded St. Petersburg as Russia's "window on Europe," an alternative to the inward-looking "Holy Russia" of Moscow. In the twentieth century, when the capital city once again became Moscow, the move symbolized a rejection of Western ways every bit as profound as Dostoevsky's rejection of the "disease" of individualism.

The clash between Dostoevsky and Turgenev was symptomatic of the profound changes taking place in Russia itself, as this backward country, which had only recently liberated the serfs, strove to enter the industrial age of nineteenth-century Europe. Dostoevsky describes the final exchange of his disastrous meeting with Turgenev: "I advised him for the sake of convenience to order a telescope from Paris. Whatever for? he asked. Russia is far from here, I replied. You would be able to train the telescope on Russia and observe us;

otherwise it really is difficult to see what is happening there. He got terribly angry."

A few months later Dostoevsky and his wife traveled to Switzerland, where they witnessed the First Congress of the League of Peace and Freedom, in Geneva. The meeting was attended by the charismatic Garibaldi, who together with his famous Redshirts had played a heroic role in the liberation of Latin America from the Spanish, and who more recently had been instrumental in the unification of Italy. Dostoevsky found himself sympathetic toward Garibaldi the man but was horrified by the ideas put forward at the congress: "the nonsense these socialists and revolutionaries talked in front of 5000 spectators is beyond belief. The bathos, feebleness, muddle, disagreements, contradictions are quite unimaginable. And this trash is agitating the unhappy working classes!" Also present at the congress was the Russian anarchist Bakunin, who had now become a major figure in the revolutionary movement. Dostoevsky had briefly met Bakunin in London during his first trip abroad in 1862, when Bakunin had just arrived in London after escaping from Siberia, and he and Dostoevsky found that they had several experiences in common. At that time Dostoevsky still had ambivalent feelings about how to alleviate the suffering of the Russian people under the autocratic regime of the tsars. Significantly, this time he made no attempt to renew his acquaintance with Bakunin, whose ideas were now anathema to him.

Dostoevsky's four-year stay in Europe was beset with financial problems. For the most part his Russian publishers sent him just enough to live on, but his recurrent obsession with gambling meant that he was constantly having to pawn his possessions or borrow from fellow Russians (he even owed fifty rubles to the despised Turgenev). As if this were not enough, Dostoevsky soon grew tired of his wife's constant company: "Always alone—we are always alone—enough to go off one's head with boredom." The strain brought on regular epileptic fits and encouraged his misanthropic inclinations. Even the inoffensive Swiss were deemed intolerable: "what self-satisfied little boasters the Swiss are . . . a sign of particular stupidity. Everywhere is horrible, rotten, and above all expensive." Worst of all, he was to be deeply affected by the death of his first-born child, his three-month-old daughter Sonya, in 1868. In the words of his wife, who was also devastated: "I was terribly afraid for my un-happy husband: his despair was stormy, he wept and sobbed like a woman as he stood before the cold body of his darling and covered her pale lit-tle face and little hands with ardent kisses. Such stormy despair I have never seen."

But most of Dostoevsky's time in Europe was spent writing, and the initial result of this was his second great masterpiece, *The Idiot*. Like all his works, both great and small, *The Idiot* is flawed—certainly more so than *Crime and Punishment*. On the other hand, it also contains writing of such power as could have been composed by no other author.

The idiot of the title is Prince Lev Nikola-evich Myshkin, a curious blend of a holy fool, a Christ-like figure, and Don Quixote. This is in many ways Dostoevsky's most spiritually ambi-tious novel. He wishes to depict a character pos-sessed by Christian goodness as he moves through a fallen secular world. Prince Myshkin is in many ways an emblem of Dostoevsky's belief in the moral qualities with which Russia could redeem the current decadence of the Western European world.

The book opens with the Warsaw express speeding through the Russian countryside toward St. Petersburg at nine o'clock on a late November morning. "It was so wet and foggy that there was still hardly any light, and from the train windows it was difficult to distinguish anything ten yards on either side of the track." In the third-class carriage: "As usual, everyone was tired, everyone's eyes were heavy from a sleepless night, everyone was chilled to the bone, everyone's face shone with the yellow pallor of the fog." Sitting by the window of the carriage was Prince Myshkin, who was returning from an extended stay at a Swiss clinic, where he had been undergoing treatment for epilepsy. His cloak was visibly inadequate against the cold, and he had only a small knotted bundle that seemed to contain all his possessions. Myshkin was "a young man of around twenty-six years old, slightly above average in height, with very thick fair hair, hollow cheeks, and a narrow, pointed almost white beard. His eyes were large and blue, and had a steady gaze, which had something heavy about it—that strange look which some people instantly recognize as that of an epileptic."

Prince Myshkin falls into conversation with a dark-haired young man in a black sheepskin coat sitting opposite him. This is Parfyon Rogozhin, who has just inherited a million rubles upon the death of his merchant father. They are joined by the smarmy, buffoon-faced Lebedev, a minor civil servant who latches onto them because he scents a chance to get hold of some of Rogozhin's money. Prince Myshkin and Rogozhin become friends, and during the course of the narrative they will both fall in love with the remarkable Natasya Filippovna, a beautiful "camellia." (This was a euphemism for a courtesan, referring to the heroine of Dumas's *The Lady of the Camellias*, which had wide currency during the period in stage and book versions as well as being the subject of Verdi's *La Traviata*.) Natasya is one of Dostoevsky's powerful yet flawed women.

She is intelligent, passionate, and possessed of her own hidden resources. Prince Myshkin is drawn to her by the inner suffering he sees in her face. She wishes to be free of the corrupt, money-grabbing world of generals and rich merchants in which she finds herself. As the novel unfolds, her special qualities as well as her hysteria become more apparent.

The giddying twists and turns of the long and convoluted plot often lead the reader far from its central narrative thread. Once again this enables us to meet a rich mix of St. Petersburg characters who exhibit the differing secular ideals, beliefs, and deceits of mid-nineteenth-century Russian urban society. This is an essentially capitalist world, motivated by greed and licentiousness.

In a dramatic climax, Natasya falls to her knees in tears before the Christ-like Prince Myshkin, trying to kiss his hand. She decides that she cannot demean Myshkin by marrying him, and deserts him. She then goes to Moscow with Rogozhin. In a memorable final scene, Prince Myshkin arrives at Rogozhin's house looking for Natasya. Rogozhin eventually lets him into the darkened apartment. Myshkin treads warily through the gloom and into the bedroom, where he makes out a body lying on the bed beneath a white sheet. The body is utterly motionless and appears to be asleep, though it is not perceptibly beathing. All around, the room is in chaos. Scraps of a torn white silk dress, lace petticoats, and ribbon are scattered about indiscriminately. On the bedside table he sees the glint of a diamond necklace, seemingly flung aside. Then, at the foot of the bed he notices a small white foot protruding from beneath a torn piece of lace. It is absolutely still and looks as if it has been sculpted out of marble. A fly buzzes above the bed. Uncorked bottles of disinfectant mask the smell. Natasya has been murdered by the insanely jealous Rogozhin.

Emotionally drained, Prince Myshkin and Rogozhin lie down together in the apartment and talk through the night. By morning Myshkin is filled with compassion and strokes Rogozhin's hair, while Rogozhin raves in his delirium. But the experience has so overwhelmed Prince Myshkin that he has suffered a mental collapse:

"Meanwhile it had become light; at last he lay down on the cushion, as though now completely powerless and in despair, and laid his face against Rogozhin's pale, motionless face; tears flowed from his eyes onto Rogozhin's cheeks, but perhaps he did not notice his own tears and was not at all aware of them."

Rozoghin will be sentenced to fifteen years in Siberia for the murder of Natasya Filippovna, and Prince Myshkin will be returned to the Swiss clinic in a state of imbecility, from which it is implied he will never recover.

What are we to make of all this? It is evident that Dostoevsky expects us once again to read a profoundly spiritual Christian message into his tale of mayhem. But by this stage his addiction to deranged characters may well have begun to obscure any message at all. Previously the characters in Dostoevsky's novels had often been deeply deprived (as in *Poor Folk*), deeply damaged (as in *House of the Dead*), or even deeply deranged (as in *The Double*), but these faults had at least been set in circumstances, or a form, in which they could be objectively judged. In *The*

Idiot the sheer torrent of hysterical, crazed, and mostly deranged characters has become overwhelming. The only way to appreciate *The Idiot* is to surrender one's rational and critical faculties, to immerse oneself entirely in its manic energy, and thus to undergo the compelling and perhaps even mildly deranging experience into which its maelstrom of hysteria and ever-shifting extremities of emotion drags the reader.

In characterizing great literature it is not customary to categorize the age at which the reader will appreciate such works. Dostoevsky would seem to be the exception that proves this rule. The earnest intensity of *The Idiot*, and to a greater or lesser extent all of his works, make such literature best appreciated in that state of bewildering emotional and philosophical intensity most frequently encountered in late teenage years. Dostoevky's works seem perfectly adapted to such intense inarticulacy, which to a certain extent they echo. This is not to belittle his achievement. It is just that at this age the true Dostoevskian experience is best appreciated.

More mature readers may experience reservations, which in the end may become insurmountable. Younger readers, in the full flush of youthful existential bewilderment, are likely to find the experience of Dostoevsky's great novels a major event of their early lives. This is prone to be a profound but not a formative event—exercising the mental and emotional faculties, yet without molding them. Few of a balanced disposition would aspire to emulate any of Dostoevsky's major characters, or even live in the world they inhabit. But immersion in such a world, for the time it takes to read several hundred pages, can be as exhilarating as any drug. And as such it lifts the reader into a world far beyond his or her normal experience. It is easy to scoff at such callow enthusiasm, but one's entry into early maturity can be distinctly lacking without having imbibed such intoxicating literary liquor.

Dostoevsky's next great novel was *The Possessed* (sometimes called *The Devils*). His novels were now becoming longer and longer, and *The Possessed* would cover seven hundred pages by the time it was finally completed in 1872, the year after the author returned to Russia from his four-year stay in Western Europe.

By now Dostoevsky's great rival Tolstoy had published his masterpiece, *War and Peace*, which had been widely acclaimed and had found a huge readership. Dostoevsky's immediate reaction had been to plan a vast work called *Atheism*, but in the end he abandoned this religious epic for an almost equally ambitious political epic in the form of *The Possessed*. This was begun in Germany around 1870. The Franco-Prussian War had broken out, throwing Europe (and Dostoevsky) into turmoil. To make matters worse, he was still prone to occasional bouts of gambling fever. (At the height of his obsession he had even pawned Anna's wedding ring as he frantically attempted to redeem his losses.) Such was the background to the beginning of his new novel.

The Possessed was initially inspired by an actual event that Dostoevsky had read about in the Russian daily papers, which he avidly devoured for news of his homeland. Late in 1869 a student called Ivanov had been found murdered in a

Moscow park. It was soon discovered that this had been the work of an underground revolutionary cell led by Sergei Nechaev, a disciple and friend of the anarchist Bakunin. Ivanov had been a disruptive member of Nechaev's clandestine group, and Nechaev had persuaded his fellow conspirators to "liquidate" him. A similar event would play a crucial role in Dostoevsky's novel.

The final version of *The Possessed* shows several signs of being a draft pieced together from several earlier drafts. The motivation of the several characters is frequently blurred as the novel powers its way through the convolutions of the plot. Likewise the first-person narrator wavers unsettlingly from intimate involvement to detached yet judgmental omniscience. Satire and comedy sit uneasily alongside desperate seriousness.

The action takes place in "a hitherto rather unremarkable town" in provincial Russia. Initially we are introduced to "the worthy Stepan Trofimovich Verkhovensky," a somewhat down-at-heel liberal with delusions of intellectual grandeur. According to the narrator, "in the late eighteen-forties, he shone briefly as a university lecturer." By the time of the novel, Verkhovensky has begun to deteriorate.

> Mr. Verkhovensky really had picked up some bad habits, particularly lately. He had become noticeably more slovenly. He drank more and had become more tearful and nervous and rather hypersensitive to aesthetic values. His face had acquired a peculiar knack of changing instantly from, say, a solemn, inspired expression to a ridiculous and even idiotic one. He couldn't bear to be left alone for a moment and constantly craved distraction.

But it appears that in Dostoevsky's eyes his main fault has been to espouse humanist ideals, question traditional ideas of right and wrong, and pay insufficient attention to his family. All this has a catastrophic effect upon his son Pyotr, as well as on Nikolay Stavrogin, who was tutored by him. The interwoven story of the latter two "devils" is the gist of *The Possessed*.

From early in his life, Stavrogin embarked upon a quest to fill the emptiness that he sensed at the center of his being. His life has consisted of a series of involvements with different ideologies, during which various characters have fallen under the influence of his powerful character.

The most negative of the "possessed" characters is the nihilist Kirillov, who is blatantly used by Dostoevsky to argue the implications following from a loss of faith in God. According to Kirillov, if God does not exist, man will have to take his place. (The outdated use of the word "man" instead of "humanity" here is all too appropriate. Throughout Dostoevsky's work, the philosophically involved part of humanity is exclusively male. His women have power, emotions, sentimentality, even understanding—as well as immense "female" strengths such as saintly qualities, irrationality, or endurance. They seldom, if ever, have ideas. And one cannot escape the suspicion that even the strongest among them remain subservient to the male-dominated ideological requirements of the plot.) Kirillov insists that if man no longer believes in God, he must grasp the utter freedom that this entails. The ultimate freedom is the choice between life and death, and Kirillov argues that it is only possible to prove that one has this freedom by gratuitously committing suicide. Only by means of this motiveless, "anti-psychological," disinterested act can we achieve our freedom.

Dostoevsky goes to some trouble to demonstrate that Kirillov is morally pure in his advocacy of such ideas, which many have seen as prophetic of the ideas that Nietzsche would advocate later in the century. This is of course nonsense. Nietzsche may have gone mad, and Kirillov is demonstratively unhinged throughout, but Nietzsche advocated neither nihilism nor suicide—quite the contrary. Admittedly, Nietzsche did stress that the individual should grasp his freedom, make his own values, and take utter responsibility for his own destiny, but this was intended to result in something more than suicide. Such is both the blatant and profound difference between Nietzsche and Dostoevsky. The latter's concern was, in the end, spiritual—involving the salvation of one's soul, regardless of the cost in life.

Another character we encounter is Shatov, who abandons his nihilist ideas to become a

Slavophile, believing in the religious mission of the Russian people. He is convinced that the Second Coming of Christ will take place in Russia. (This was a barely exaggerated view of Dostoevsky's convictions.)

The second main strain of the narrative involves Pyotr Verkhovensky, the son of the decrepit humanist Stepan Verkhovensky, who has been deranged by his liberal upbringing. Pyotr is the leader of the band of revolutionary conspirators who make up the rest of the "possessed" (or devils) of the title. (It is necessary to bear in mind both aspects. Dostoevsky makes it plain that it is only because they are possessed by such evil ideas that they become devils. In the prologue to the novel he specifically quotes the biblical story of the Gadarene swine, where Jesus encounters a man possessed by devils. "Then he cast out the devils from the man, and they entered into the herd of swine, and the herd rushed down the steep slope into the lake where they were drowned.") In an echo of the original Moscow murder that had inspired this work, Pyotr plans to murder Shatov, an act that he believes will bind his fellow revolutionaries together. But the murder has unforeseen effects. Eventually Kirillov travesties his so-called ideals by falsely confessing to the murder of Shatov. This is both something less than suicide as well as something less than disinterested, for it has a very palpable motive.

There is no need to attach specific ideas to Dostoevsky's conspirators, be they Nietzschean, revolutionary Marxist, anarchist, or what have you. No matter how crazed, nihilistic, or even plain contradictory the ideas in the novel may appear, they are in fact utterly plausible within their own context. They are also extremely relevant to the terrorist-plagued world in which we find ourselves today. Dostoevsky's conception, his "possessed" minds, are no more or less than archetypal terrorists. His great imaginative leap was to show precisely how terrorists thought. Here were their inconsistent motives, whether the group regarded itself as religious or nihilist. This was the way they operated; this was the way they saw the world *no matter what they believed*. In a prophetically impressive moment,

Pyotr Verkhovensky claims that when the revolution is fully achieved, "Cicero will have his tongue cut out, Copernicus will have his eyes put out, Shakespeare will be stoned." All this will happen in the name of "equality." No one familiar with twentieth-century Russian history could fail to recognize such a situation. In this way *The Possessed* is highly prescient of the revolution that created the Soviet state, which would take place less than half a century after this work was written. More than this, it is also prescient of our world today. Fundamental terrorists will always have the same attitude toward Cicero, Copernicus, and Shakespeare—voices that speak for a world free from terror.

Dostoevsky's *The Possessed* may be prophetic, but that does not mean it is in any way a coherent, satisfying, or even convincing work of literature. As a handbook for government agents involved in anti-terrorist activity, it should be compulsory reading. Dostoevsky's insights into the conspiratorial mind have been forgotten, learned, and forgotten again throughout the long years since the book's publication. Anyone wishing to understand the terrorist mind has no need of interrogation transcripts from Guantanamo Bay, and any blurred message they might convey. People seeking coherent reasons for suicide bombers need look no further than Kirillov's cogent but essentially self-contradictory self-justifications. Here in *The Possessed* we find conveyed the true motive that lies above and beyond any apparent idealism which the perpetrator himself may be persuaded is his "real" reason for his actions. Such is the power of Dostoevsky's insight into the extremist mind—or perhaps, in his case, the mind at its extremes.

This may well be, but as literature *The Possessed* has deep flaws. Here again Dostoevsky indulges in a favorite device which became increasingly evident in his mature work. Characters are described in a few lines of physical detail as soon as they appear. After this, virtually no reference is made to the character's appearance. He becomes for the most part merely a voice, swapping chunks of frantic dialogue with other similarly described characters. These conversations are accompanied by occasional dramatic gestures, but these are in no way integrated into a coherent personality. In *The Possessed* the characters tend only to take on a certain personality through their crazed behavior and evil nature. But then most of the characters exhibit these qualities to a greater or lesser degree. There are no counterbalancing "good" characters.

A period of relief in *The Possessed* is provided by the unfortunate Karmazinov, who is described as "an old man with a rather red face, thick grey locks of hair clustering under his chimney-pot hat and curling round his clean little pink ears. Tortoise-shell lorgnette, on a narrow black ribbon, studs, buttons, signet-ring, all in the best form. A sugary but rather shrill voice." Indicatively, this hurried description is set down almost in note form. It is intended as a caricature of Dostoevsky's old enemy Turgenev (to whom he *still* owed fifty rubles). Dostoevsky "satirically" describes how Karmazinov hobnobs with the revolutionaries who seek to destroy his country while at the same time selling his assets in Russia so that he can take up permanent residence in Germany. Humor in Dostoevsky is for the most part heavily loaded—either satirical or tending to ridicule. Like his dialogue, it appears to take place in a world requiring frequent exclamation points.

The novel also includes a particularly unsavory episode, known as "Stavrogin's Confession," which was omitted from early editions. In this, Stavrogin describes how he raped a fourteen-year-old girl. *The Possessed* finally comes to an end when Stavrogin hangs himself. Its last words are: "After the autopsy, all our medical experts rejected any possibility of insanity." How much we choose to believe this of Stavrogin, or any of the other characters, is a matter of taste.

In 1873 Dostoevsky became editor of *The Citizen*, a magazine with a distinctly conservative outlook. To this he contributed a column entitled "The Diary of a Writer." Owing to the enormous popular success of this column, he eventually made it into a magazine of his own—which he published, edited, and filled exclusively with his own writing. This brought Dostoevsky to the notice of an even wider public, and he gradually assumed the public role of Russia's great writer.

This was, and would remain until well into the twentieth century, a figure of peculiar stature, involving in differing degrees elements of prophet, social seer, and a quasi-religious conception of the role of the artist. (In the twentieth century this role would be taken on by Pasternak and to a certain degree by Solzhenitsyn. The composer Shostakovich also occupied a similar role. Significantly, no Russian dictator ever ventured to murder these figures, who were permitted to function with a degree of freedom *in vacuo*, so to speak. The works produced in this vacuum, which subsequently became public, fully justified their author's strange and difficult role—as if the incumbents knew what was *expected* of them according to this curious tradition. The classic twentieth-century example of such a work is *Dr. Zhivago*.)

In *The Diary of a Writer,* Dostoevsky included short stories, notes, semi-fictional sketches, psychological analyses of the latest sensational murder cases, philosophical musings, and his ever-developing religio-political views, which now became right wing in the extreme. By this time the countries of Western Europe were developing industrially and economically into recognizable modern societies. Dostoevsky saw this as evidence of terminal decline. He prophesied to his readers that Western Europe would soon collapse. This would be followed by a period during which the prophecies in the biblical Book of Revelations would finally come to pass. Holy Russia, in which the Orthodox church would reign supreme, would then become the Kingdom of God on Earth.

At the same time Dostoevsky was penning his religious pipe dreams, remarkably similar political fantasies were being penned in London by Karl Marx, who had published *Das Kapital* in 1867, almost coinciding with *The Idiot*. Marx's dream, which was not in any way specially tailored to Russian circumstances, would nonetheless be realized there after 1917. What is remarkable is the uncanny resemblance between the Russian interpretation of Marx's concepts and Dostoevsky's apocalyptic ideas. In both creeds, Russia was to be Heaven on Earth—with only a strictly orthodox/Orthodox interpretation of this state of affairs permitted. Even the anti-Semitic and anti-Catholic elements of Soviet Russia were already present in some of the more notorious passages of *The Diary of a Writer*. Despite such crass notions, Dostoevsky's quasi-journalistic output enabled him to develop to the full the more philosophical ideas that would emerge in their final form in his next great novel, *The Brothers Karamazov*. This, his final work, is generally regarded by his aficionados as his finest. Despite his handicapping belief in so much extreme right-wing nonsense, the writer in him shone through. Dostoevsky conclusively proved that he was still capable of producing great literature, albeit of an overwhelmingly Dostoevskian tenor.

The Brothers Karamazov is, in many versions, over a thousand pages long, yet Dostoevsky managed to complete it in just two years, working throughout 1879 until the end of 1880. Its style betrays much evidence of having been written at this frantic pace. In many places the dialogue is headlong, pouring from the characters at great speed, often as if gabbled. Sometimes, in the most commonplace discussions, it is merely disjointed: "I hope he doesn't turn up. That would be splendid. You don't suppose I like all this disgusting business of yours, do you? And with you here, too? So we'll come to dinner." As for the setting of such "conversations": these barely exist. Descriptions of the natural world, houses and monasteries (interior or exterior), changes of expression on the faces of the particulars, subtle nuances of light and shade—such things are consumed in the white heat of Dostoevsky's confrontations and everything that he is so desperate to *say*. As his fellow Russian Nabokov put it: "The weather does not exist in his world, so it does not much matter how people dress." This might not be such a failing in a country of uniform temperate climate. In a land where winter regularly registers temperatures of minus 22 degrees Fahrenheit and summer temperatures can reach 104 degrees, such things as clothes and weather tend to be important. They also help the reader visualize the scenes. A character swaddled like an Inuit somehow evokes a very different reaction from one dressed only in a straw hat and shorts. Devoid of background or foreground, Dostoevsky's landscape is an inner climate and terrain, a mental backdrop enclosing the naked psychology of his "characters." Lightning bolts and rare calms of emotion accompany thunderous assertions about sinners, murder, the heights of spirituality, evil, and so forth. Dostoevsky's final epic novel does not so much create a world as a meteorology of extreme mental climates. On the other hand, enthusiastic readers may find themselves transported into a realm where passionate moral forces combine to enact a drama of desolate grandeur. Reactions to Dostoevsky are invariably as extreme as the conflicts he describes. There is little room for lukewarm response or nitpicking literary assessment.

In *The Brothers Karamazov*, Dostoevsky makes things plain from the outset: the novel is set in the provincial town of Skotoprigonyevsk, which in Russian means "beast pen" or "animal enclosure." The story is of the dramatic events marking the decline of the local Karamazov family. "Kara" means black in Turkish, and Dostoevsky appears to have used this covert reference as a constant reminder concerning the nature of this family while he was writing the book. The head of the family is Fyodor Pavlovich Karamazov, a degenerate landowner who spends most of his time galavanting, playing the buffoon, and scoffing at lofty ideals. His abrasiveness and his drunkenness are offset only by a certain comic element, which is intended to introduce an endearing aspect to this otherwise repulsive character. Fyodor was "all his life the most voluptuous-tempered of men, reaching in a trice to cling to any skirt at all, no sooner did it lead him on." He has been married twice and has three legitimate sons—the "brothers Karamazov" of the title: Dmitry, Ivan, and Alyosha. His servant Smerdyakov is his illegitimate offspring, conceived as a result of a bet which Fyodor Karamazov won by raping the mentally deficient waif "stinking Lizaveta."

Fyodor's first wife Adelaida had been a beautiful young heiress who eloped with him, only to be disillusioned and cheated out of her 25,000-ruble inheritance. She was the mother of Fyodor's first son, Dmitry, and eventually ran off with a graduate from a religious seminary. Fyodor's second marriage had been to a sixteen-year-old orphan, Sophia, who had soon been driven to attempt suicide and had eventually died. She had given birth to Ivan and Alyosha. Fyodor had grotesquely neglected his three young sons, using the family home for his drunken orgies with prostitutes. The sons had largely been brought up by servants and distant relatives, and had grown up estranged from their father.

The narrative begins with a family meeting that has been arranged at the local monastery. By now the members of the family scarcely know one another, and the meeting has been arranged to settle their differences. The brothers have grown up separately, and their father is by now a drunken wreck, a parody of licentiousness with his blubbery lips and stumps of black teeth. He has perversely chosen the monastery as their meeting place because his son Alyosha is a novice there, and has by now become a favorite of Zossima, the monastery's "Holy Elder" and a man of saintly wisdom. Fyodor Karamozov soon ensures that the family meeting degenerates into a scandalous farce. He mimics the behavior of the others and even mocks the venerable Zossima, kneeling before him and asking how he can get into heaven. He disingenuously suggests to his sons that he is behaving in this way only to put Zossima's spiritual qualities to the test. Zossima is by now very ill, almost certainly dying, but he benignly attempts to humor Fyodor Karamazov. At the same time he sees through Fyodor's behavior, admonishing him to stop telling lies.

The novel then moves on through a series of counterbalancing scenes. This overbearing neatness of plot is fortunately obscured by the unbalanced characters who inhabit these scenes. The "heroes" of this vast, rambling novel are the three Karamazov brothers, who are each intended to represent an aspect of humanity. Dmitry embodies the emotions, Alyosha embodies faith, and Ivan is the beleaguered representative of reason.

Dmitry is an army officer, given to "spontaneous" and spendthrift behavior. His open heart is capable of both passionate and spiritual love. He can apparently worship "Sodom" and a "Madonna" simultaneously. These aspects of his life are represented by Grushenka and Katerina. The noble Katerina entrusts Dmitry with three thousand rubles, which he promptly fritters away. Despite, or perhaps because, of this, Dmitry's sadistic behavior toward her causes her to fall in love with him. Grushenka, on the other hand, is yet another example of Dostoevsky's "fallen" women; she eventually reveals her redeeming spiritual qualities by her loyalty to Dmitry. His father is also after Grushenka and intends to bribe her with three thousand rubles to surrender herself to him. Not surprisingly, Dmitry develops a murderous hatred of his father.

When the disgusting old man is eventually murdered, Dostoevsky ensures that all the circumstantial evidence points to Dmitry having committed parricide. Among this evidence are three thousand rubles which he is supposed to have stolen from his father. For some reason Dostoevsky seems to have become obsessed with the sum of three thousand rubles, which crops up in this novel in the most unexpected places—including the extra money Fyodor Karamazov hopes to make on the sale of a wood, and the fee required by the St. Petersburg lawyer for defending Dmitry at his trial. This sum can hardly be viewed as a leitmotif, as it sometimes has relevance, sometimes has none. Even persistent sleuthing by Dostoevsky's biographers has failed to unearth any convincing reason why this particular sum should continue to buzz so persistently in his brain during this period of feverish literary activity.

The other two brothers Karamazov, Ivan and Alyosha, act as a foil toward each other. Alyosha is another of Dostoevsky's Christ-like figures. His spiritual mentor is the aged Zossima, whose holiness and wisdom are such that on occasion he can see into the souls of others. At one point Zossima prostrates himself before Dmitry because he can see that Dmitry will soon be undergoing great suffering. Dostoevsky would have us believe that the holy Alyosha is the main hero of the novel, but this role is undoubtedly usurped by the devilishly brilliant Ivan. On a number of occasions in the novel, Ivan uses the full and ingenious powers of his considerable intellect to prove that the God he does not wish to believe in does not exist. Here Dostoevsky's penchant for masochism reaches new spiritual heights. Despite being a fervent believer, he proceeds to invent—and place in Ivan's mouth—several powerfully convincing arguments against the existence of God. One of these, Dostoevsky confessed in a letter to a friend, he found utterly unanswerable. He could not understand how God permitted the suffering of innocent children in the universe over which He ruled. Yet Dostoevsky remained a firm believer nonetheless.

Like Prince Myshkin, Alyosha also has his human side. Perhaps owing to his innocent youth, he does succumb to moments of earthly temptation—particularly to lust, a subject that always remained close to Dostoevsky's heart. At one point in the Karamazov saga, a gossipy character called Rakitin, whose spiritual qualities are quite evidently viewed by the author as beneath contempt, tries to put the inexperienced Alyosha right about sex. He explains that a man is capable of throwing away everything he has in his lust for a woman's body, though this desire is in fact only for one particular part of a woman's body. We evidently need to be informed of this just as much as the callow Alyosha, as an integral part of our thousand-page spiritual voyage to redemption.

Ivan is the most intriguing of the brothers, a solitary character driven by an intellectual passion. Even his father Fyodor declares, "He's not one of us." When questioned about his beliefs, he insists that he has a "Euclidian mind." He believes in reason and geometry, though he is unable to comprehend how two parallel lines meet at infinity, as they do according to the fifth postulate of Euclid's geometry. (Here Ivan seems to be confusing the ideas of mathematical and theological infinity.) Ivan argues his case against God with great ingenuity, and in so doing puts his brother Alyosha's faith to supreme test. In fact it is suggested that his aim is not to undermine his brother's faith; he is covertly hoping that Alyosha will provide him with a reason for believing in God.

Ivan's most powerful arguments against God are presented in the chapter known as "The Grand Inquisitor," which is said to be Ivan's "poem." This chapter recounts how Christ returned briefly to earth in the sixteenth century during the Spanish Inquisition in Seville. "He came down into the hot 'streets and lanes' of the southern city just at the moment when, a day before, nearly a hundred heretics had been burnt all at once by the cardinal, the Grand Inquisitor." Christ performs a miracle, healing a blind man, and then resurrects a seven-year-old girl from her coffin. The latter miracle is witnessed by the Grand Inquisitor, who is described as "an old man of nearly ninety, tall and erect, with a shriveled face and sunken eyes, from which, though, a light like a fiery spark still gleams." The Grand Inquisitor orders the guards to seize Christ and decides that he will be burnt at the stake as "the vilest of heretics."

The essential passage of "The Grand Inquisitor" involves the Inquisitor himself confronting Christ. His main complaint is that Christ has overestimated humanity's capacity for free will. Christ's aim was to liberate humanity, but humanity did not wish to face the agony of free choice. Instead, humanity preferred security, certainty, and spiritual ease. Only the few have the strength to take on the responsibility of freedom. The rest are content to surrender their freedom to the church, allowing it to have the power to tell them how to behave.

Alyosha recognizes that Ivan is describing the Roman Catholic church, which behaves like a state power, whereas in the true church each individual takes on his own freedom, and the state withers away. (Coincidentally, Marx claimed that precisely this would happen when true communism was finally achieved.)

Ivan's arguments against God are meant to be part of his spiritual struggle. Zossima, who remains the fountain of true wisdom, sees that Ivan is on a "pilgrimage" to "higher things." Although ironically, many later critics would ignore the place of God altogether in Dostoevsky's arguments. For them, humanity's responsibility for its own freedom was the main concern. In stressing that humanity should face up to its agonizing freedom of choice, Dostoevsky was here laying the foundations of existentialism. At the same time he was writing *The*

Brothers Karamazov, the ideas of the Danish philosopher-theologian Søren Kierkegaard were beginning to spread through Europe and into Russia. Kierkegaard put forward a remarkably similar argument concerning humanity's ultimate responsibility to itself, which he also argued as a reason for spiritual commitment to God. As such, Dostoevsky and Kierkegaard are now seen as the forerunners of twentieth-century European existentialism—despite the fact that this philosophy largely took on a humanistic, atheistic approach. The freedom was accepted, but it also allowed us to *reject* God. Existentialism taught that each individual must recognize the tremendous responsibility that this freedom places on his life. In choosing, we choose ourselves. Freedom is the essential part of the human condition, from which we cannot absolve ourselves. Anyone who does not face up to this situation is acting in "bad faith." It is only by choosing our freedom that we create ourselves. It is not difficult to see how such "godless" ideas developed from the "God-obsessed" ideas of Dostoevsky.

Later in *The Brothers Karamazov*, when Ivan is becoming (even more) deranged, he has a nightmare in which he encounters the Devil, and together they have a remarkably civilized philosophical discussion. In a particularly original touch, Dostoevsky chooses to represent the Devil as a slightly down-at-heel fellow: "his linen was rather dirty and the wide scarf very threadbare. The visitor's check trousers were of an excellent cut, but again were a little too light in color, such, in fact, as were no longer worn." In fact the Devil comes across as "a sort of well-bred sponger, who was dependent upon his kind old friends."

During the long discussion between Ivan and the Devil, it emerges that the Devil keeps abreast of all the latest intellectual fashions. He refers to Ivan Karamazov's ideas about "the new men . . . who propose to destroy everything and start with cannibalism." He recalls how Ivan was highly irritated by these people, believing them all to be fools. They had not the first idea how to go about such things. If only they had asked him, Ivan, he would have set them right. There was no need to destroy everything and return to a primitive state of cannibalism in order to achieve a new order of things. All that was needed was to destroy "the idea of God in humanity." This alone would be sufficient to bring about "a new era." Then men would unite together at last, to bring about joy and happiness on earth. Everyone would finally realize that he had only one life and would accept the fact that he was mortal. Yet this very consciousness of life's momentary nature would "intensify its fire to the same extent as it is now dissipated in the hopes of eternal life beyond the grave."

During the twentieth century, both Communists and capitalists would in their own way recognize this state of humanity. As far as capitalism and liberal democracy are concerned, this remains very much our secular view of life on earth. For Dostoevsky, this was the evil Ivan Karamazov's view of the future—which the Devil welcomed: "If it comes, everything is resolved and mankind will attain its goal," though he considered that "it may not be attained for a thousand years." Yet as we have seen, for Dostoevsky himself salvation lay elsewhere, in a less rosy future.

In the end it emerges that Fyodor Karamazov has been murdered by his illegitimate son Smerdyakov. Despite this, Dmitry is tried, found guilty, and sentenced to Siberia. This can be understood as Dostoevsky's way of suggesting that regardless of what happens, we are all in fact guilty. In order to redeem himself, Dmitry must undergo his experience of purgatory—from which, it is more than hinted, he will emerge as a finer human being.

By the end of the 1870s even the comparatively liberal rule of Alexander II was faced with revolutionary unrest in Russia. From exile, Bakunin advocated banditry as "one of the most honorable forms of Russian folk life." In April 1879 an assassin attempted to shoot Alexander II as he was taking his morning walk. Ten months later the tsar's residence was dynamited and he escaped assassination only because he was late for dinner. Dostoevsky supported the government but found himself in a quandary. The prospects for Russia looked bleak.

In June 1880 a monument to Russia's greatest poet, Pushkin, was unveiled in Moscow. As part of the celebrations marking this event, Dostoevsky delivered a speech in which he sought to heal the growing rifts in Russian society. Yet for him this did not involve a reconciliation between conservative and socialist elements. Far from it. Socialism and revolution were anathema to him. The only way to avoid Russia falling into the grip of such forces lay in the "fraternal harmony of all tribes under Christ's evangelical law." Instead of socialism, Russians should adopt "humble association with the common people."

The fervor with which Dostoevsky delivered this speech stirred those who heard it to wild enthusiasm. According to one report, the large audience in the Hall of Columns was "transformed by the voice of genius." Other, more sober reports realized that Dostoevsky was now completely out of touch with the realities of the difficult contemporary situation in Russia. Whatever the answer to Russia's problems, it did not lie in transforming the country into some mythical Kingdom of God on Earth.

This was to be the fifty-nine-year-old Dostoevsky's last appearance in public. By now his lifelong heavy smoking had given him emphysema, and the strain of constant overwork meant that he was subject to increasingly regular epileptic fits. In November 1880 he finally completed *The Brothers Karamazov*, and within two months he was on his deathbed. On the morning of Wednesday, January 28, 1881, he asked for his Bible. His wife Anna laid it before him, and he opened it at random, according to the Russian superstition, to see what it prophesied. Anna read to him the words he had found, and he said, "This means I am going to die." By the evening he was dead. Three days later, despite the extreme cold of the Russian midwinter, thirty thousand people lined the streets of St. Petersburg to watch his coffin pass. The speeches at his graveside are said to have lasted six hours.

Afterword

Dostoevsky's great novels burst upon the European literary scene like a succession of thunderbolts. Over the next decades their raw psychology and passionate involvement had a galvanizing effect upon writers and thinkers as disparate as Nietzsche and Kafka. The study of human psychology was entering a new phase, and Dostoevsky's understanding of the darker and more extreme recesses of the human mind cast a light into areas that had seldom been illuminated with such force since the ancient Greek tragedies and Shakespeare.

As psychological art, Dostoevsky's novels stand in the stark tradition originated by

Sophocles' Oedipus plays. Yet as literature they have met with a more ambivalent response. After the initial blinding shock of recognition, some critics began on second glance to detect a more threadbare element. Dostoevsky's powerful effects were supported by a rather ramshackle structure. Both sanity and literary art were sometimes in short supply.

Basically, this critical ambivalence may be summarized, as it was by the leading twentieth-century critic George Steiner, as "Tolstoy or Dostoevsky?" Dostoevsky was a titan, flinging down lightning from his clouded spiritual Olympus. His political-religious novels sought to wean the soul of man from the nihilistic ideas that threatened to transform him forever from a religion-oriented being to a purely secular entity. Tolstoy was the master of a more civilized tradition. His two great social-   ical novels, *War and Peace* and *Anna K*   represent the twin peaks of a European cultural tradition. They are the acme of the novel, demonstrating all that it can contain (including the soulful aspect so beloved of Dostoevsky). Beside the sym-

100

phonic magnificence of Tolstoy's masterpieces, Dostoevsky's great works appear like a hell's choir of harpies and devils. Not for one moment does one doubt their integrity, yet compared with Tolstoy and other great European novelists, one cannot but notice Dostoevsky's crudity. Such lack of artistic finesse is not excused by the force of his religious and Slavophile enthusiasms, his underlying obsession with "Holy Russia," and the souls of his frequently unhinged characters. This is not simply a matter of misunderstanding Dostoevsky's "Russianness." His fellow Russian Nabokov deplores Dostoevsky's "lack of taste, his monotonous dealings with persons suffering from pre-Freudian complexes, the way he has of wallowing in the tragic misadventures of human dignity."

Dostoevsky's lapses of artistry and taste are undeniable. But is this a fatal flaw? Anyone who has ever found themselves swept along by the full force of Dostoevsky's hectic words, allowing themselves to be carried willy-nilly on the torrent of the headlong narrative—the breathless dialectic conversations, the impetuous gestures, the dramatic consequences—will never forget this intoxicating feeling. And, as I suggested earlier, this experience may well be best achieved in late youth or early manhood, or their female equivalent. Seen in this light, Dostoevsky's achievement may not be universal, but a great achievement it remains, even in such limited company. His work is not so much literature as raw spiritual experience, and as such is best experienced at that age when existential questions (with or without belief in God) are most pressing, when our entire future life seems to depend—as well it might—upon the decisions we make, upon whom we find ourselves to be, and whom we decide we wish to become.

From Dostoevsky's Writings

From Crime and Punishment. *Raskolnikov is in Siberia, and has a meeting with Sonya:*

As Raskolnikov sat idly gazing before him, his thoughts passed into daydreams, and then contemplation. He thought of nothing in particular, but found himself troubled and excited by an unplaceable restlessness. Suddenly he found that Sonya was beside him. She had approached noiselessly and sat at his side. It was still quite early, and the morning chill remained sharp. She was wearing her ragged old cloak and was wrapped in her green shawl. Her face still betrayed signs of her past illness; it was thinner and paler. She gave her usual joyful smile at seeing him, but held out her hand toward him with her customary timidity. She was always timid about offering her hand to him, and sometimes did not offer it at all, as if she were afraid he might reject it. . . . Yet now their hands did not part. He stole a quick glance at her, and dropped his eyes to the ground without speaking. They were alone. No one had seen them. The guard was looking elsewhere.

How it happened he never knew. All of a sudden something seemed to seize him and fling him down at her feet. He went and threw his arms around her knees. For the first few moments she was terribly frightened and turned even paler. She leapt to her feet and trembled as she looked down at him. Yet at the same moment she understood, and a light of infinite joy came into her eyes. She understood beyond all doubt that he loved her beyond everything and that at last the moment had come. . . .

They wanted to speak, but could not. There were tears in their eyes. They were both pale and thin; but those sickly pale faces were bright with the dawn of a new future, of a full resurrection into a new life. . . . They resolved to wait and be patient. They had a full seven years to wait, though what terrible suffering and infinite happiness lay before them until then!

From Notes from the Underground. *The celebrated opening passage, in which one of the first existential heroes introduces himself:*

I am a sick man. . . . I am an angry man. I am an unattractive man. I think there is something wrong with my liver. But I don't understand the first thing about my illness, and I don't even know for certain which part of me is affected. I am not having any treatment for it, never have had, although I have nothing but respect for medicine and for doctors. I am, besides, extremely superstitious, if only because I have such respect for medicine. (I am well educated enough not to be superstitious, but I am superstitious nonetheless.) No, I refuse to be treated out of spite. You probably won't be able to understand that. But I understand it. I can't really explain who my spite is directed against, in this matter; I am perfectly well aware that I can't get one over on the doctors in any way by not consulting them; I am perfectly well aware that I'm harming no one but myself by doing this. When all's said and done, the reason I don't have any treatment is out of spite. Is my liver out of order?—let it get worse!

From The Possessed. *The notorious passage known as "Stavrogin's Confession," in which he confesses what he did to the fourteen-year-old Matryosha:*

Matryosha sat in her room, on a bench, with her back to me, going about her sewing. After a while, she suddenly burst into song, singing very softly, as she often did. I took out my watch and looked at the time: it was two o'clock. My heart began beating. I got up and began approaching her stealthily. The pots of geraniums stood on the windowsill, and the sun shone very brightly. I quietly sat down beside her on the floor. She started, and at first appeared frightened and jumped up. I took her hand and kissed it gently, sat her down on the bench, and began looking into her eyes. My kissing of her hand made her suddenly laugh, like a baby, but only for a moment, because she then jumped up impetuously a second time and was so frightened that a spasm passed across her face. She looked at me with eyes motionless with terror, and her lips began to twitch as if she were on the point of crying, but she didn't cry. I kissed her hand again and took her on my knee. Then she quickly pulled herself away and smiled, as if she were ashamed. I was whispering to her all the while, as if I was drunk. Suddenly a strange thing happened, which I will never forget, which completely flummoxed me. The little girl wrapped her arms around my neck and began kissing me passionately. Her face appeared ecstatic. I almost got up and went away— I felt filled with pity because it was so unpleasant for me that a young child should behave like this.

When it was all over, she was confused. I didn't try to reassure her and no longer fondled her. She looked at me, smiling timidly. Her face suddenly appeared so stupid. With each passing moment she appeared to become increasingly confused. In the end she covered her face with her hands and stood in the corner motionless with her face to the wall. I was afraid she might become frightened again, like she had before, and I silently crept out of the house.

From The Idiot. *Toward the end of the novel, the Prince arrives at Rogozhin's home and demands to see Natasya Filippovna. Rogozhin shows him into a darkened room:*

But now his eyes had become so accustomed to the general gloom that he could distinguish through the darkness a bed. Someone was asleep upon it—sleeping an absolutely motionless sleep. Not the slightest movement was perceptible, not the faintest breathing was distinguishable. The sleeper was covered in a white sheet. . . . All around, on the bed, on the chair beside it, were scattered the different portions of a magnificent white silk dress, bits of lace, and rich ribbon. On a small table by the pillow glittered a mass of diamonds, torn off and thrown down anyhow. From under a heap of lace at the end of the bed peeped one small white foot, which looked as though it had been chiseled out of marble; terribly, dreadfully still and white it seemed.

The Prince gazed and gazed, and felt that the more he gazed the more deadly became the silence. Suddenly a fly awoke somewhere and buzzed across the room, hovered over the bed, and settled in silence on the pillow. The Prince shuddered. . . .

"I see you are shuddering," said Rogozhin eventually. . . .

The Prince bent forward to listen, putting all the strain he could muster upon his understanding in order to take in what Rogozhin said, and continuing to gaze questioningly at the latter's face.

"Did you do that?" he said softly, motioning with his head.

"Yes, I did it," whispered Rogozhin, and then sank into silence.

Neither man spoke for five minutes.

From The Brothers Karamazov. *Ivan's nightmare, when he speaks with the Devil:*

"Shut up! Or I'll kill you!" shouted Ivan.

"Kill me? No, I must have my say," insisted his visitor. "That's why I am here. Oh, I so love the dreams of my passionate young friends, who crave for life! 'There are new men,' you told yourself last spring, when you were about to visit here, 'who intend to destroy everything and start again with cannibalism. What fools! Why didn't they ask my advice? There's no need to destroy everything and begin all over again as cannibals. All that needs to be destroyed is the idea of God in mankind. That's where we ought to start. . . . Once the whole of mankind renounces God—and this, like the successive geological ages, will come to pass—the entire old outlook on life will collapse of its own accord, and so will the old morality. Then a new era can begin. Men will join together to obtain everything that life can give, but only for joy and happiness in this world alone. Man will become exalted with a divine spirit, his insurmountable

110

pride, and this man-god will walk the earth. Hour by hour he will extend his conquest over nature, making equal use of his will and science. Mankind will understand that it is mortal, that there is no life to come, and he will accept death with pride and good grace like a god. . . .' How charming! . . . But the question is, you now wondered, whether such an age will ever come. For if it comes, everything is resolved and mankind will achieve his ultimate goal."

From The Diary of a Writer. *Dostoevsky delivers his ideas on "Europe" under a section entitled "Servility or Politeness?":*

It is known that all educated Russians are extremely polite—that is, whenever they deal with Europe, or they think they are being looked at by Europeans, even though they are not being looked at at all. Oh, at home on our own home ground, we'll have it our way—at home such Europeanism can be dropped. Let's take as an example, say, our family relationships, our attitude—in the overwhelming majority of instances—toward civic matters such as honor and duty. All right, who among all our "preachers" who recommend "European" ideas really believes in them? Of course, only honest men, and of course only kindhearted men, who believe in them precisely because they are kindhearted. But how many such men do we have in our country?

Strictly speaking, perhaps, there isn't a single European among us, quite simply because we're not capable of being Europeans. In Russia, progressive intellectuals, and those who haunt the stock exchange, indeed our leading minds, they all pay lip service to European ideas. And in my opinion it's the same everywhere. Of course, I am not referring to people who are possessed of common sense: they don't believe in European ideas, because quite simply there's nothing to believe in. Nothing in the world was ever so obscure, vague, uncertain and indefinable as that "*body of ideas*" which we have managed to accumulate during our two centuries of Europeanism. In essence, it is no such thing as a body—merely a chaos of dismembered and disjointed bits and pieces, of alien sentiments and unintelligible ideas, of habits and words. Particularly words, words, words—of course they are the most liberal and European of words, but as far as we are concerned, nothing but words.

Dostoevsky's Chief Works in English Translation

When looking up Dostoevsky, remember that our English spelling is taken from the Russian cyrillic. This has resulted in several phonetic versions, including Dostoyevsky, Dostoevski, Dostoievski, and other more exotic variants.

Poor Folk (1846)[†]
The Double (1846)[*][†]
House of the Dead (1862)[*][†]
The Insulted and the Injured (1862)
Notes from the Underground (1864)[*][†]

[*]starred entries indicate major works
[†]indicates work discussed in the text

The Gambler (1866)[†]
Crime and Punishment (1866)[*][†]
The Eternal Husband (1870)
The Possessed (also known as *The Devils*) (1871)[*][†]
A Raw Youth (1875)
The Dream of a Ridiculous Man (1877)
The Brothers Karamazov (1880)[*][†]
The Diary of a Writer (1880)[†]

Chronology of
Dostoevsky's Life and Times

1821	Fyodor Mikhailovich Dostoevsky born November 11 (October 30 Old Style) at Mariinski Hospital in Moscow.
1821	Dostoevsky's father buys Darovoe country estate in Tula district.
1826	The Russian mathematician Lobachevsky announces new non-Euclidian geometry.
1825	Decembrist uprising: widespread revolt among young officers against tsarist repression.
1834	Dostoevsky goes to private school in Moscow.

1837	Mother dies. Dostoevsky joins his brother Mikhail at Academy of Military Engineering in St. Petersburg. Death of Pushkin in duel.
1839	Dostoevsky's father is murdered by his serfs on estate at Darovoe.
1841	Gogol publishes *Dead Souls*.
1843	Dostoevsky graduates from military academy and begins one year's military service.
1844	Dostoevsky resigns commission and leaves army to devote himself to writing in St. Petersburg.
1846	Publication of *Poor Folk* to critical acclaim from Belinsky. Publication of *The Double* disappoints critics.
1846–1847	Estrangement from Belinsky Circle. Begins to attend meetings of Petrashevsky Circle.
1848	Revolutionary uprisings in cities throughout Europe.
1849	Dostoevsky arrested by tsarist political police. Interrogated by General

	Nabokov in Peter and Paul Fortress. Undergoes mock execution before being sent to Siberia.
1850–1854	Dostoevsky serves penal servitude at Tobolsk, Siberia.
1851	Opening of Moscow-to-St. Petersburg railway.
1835–1856	Crimean War.
1855	Death of Nicholas I and succession of more enlightened Alexander II.
1854–1875	Dostoevsky serves as private in the army at Semipalatinsk.
1857–1859	Serves as lieutenant in the army. Marries widow Maria Dimitriyevna.
1860–1862	Publication of *House of the Dead*.
1861	Emancipation of the serfs. Outbreak of American Civil War.
1864	Death of Dostoevsky's wife Maria and his elder brother Mikhail. Publication of *Notes from the Undergound*.
1866	Dostoevsky publishes *The Gambler* and *Crime and Punishment*.

1867	Marx completing *Das Kapital*; Dostoevsky completing *The Idiot*. Marriage to second wife, Anna Grigoryevna.
1867–1871	Dostoevsky and his new wife live in Western Europe.
1868	Tolstoy publishes *War and Peace*.
1870	Birth of Lenin.
1871	Mendeleyev publishes Periodic Table of the Chemical Elements. Paris Commune: first Communist revolution in Europe.
1872	Marx's *Das Kapital* published in Russia.
1878	Tolstoy publishes *Anna Karenina*.
1879	Birth of Stalin.
1880	Dostoevsky delivers "Pushkin Speech," completes *The Brothers Karamazov*.
1881	Death of Dostoevsky, January 28. Assassination of Alexander II; succession of Alexander III begins period of repression.

Recommended Reading

Anna Dostoevsky, *Dostoevsky: Reminiscences* (Liveright, 1975). A fascinating, intimate portrait of the great writer by his second wife, who lived with him through the trials and tribulations of his periods in Europe at the casinos, and during the composition of several of his greatest masterpieces.

Fyodor Dostoevsky, *The Gambler*, translated by Victor Terras (University of Chicago Press, 1972). Besides containing Dostoevsky's most frantic autobiographical novel, this edition also includes a rare gem: Polina Suslova's diary. Suslova may have been a minor writer, but she offers a fascinating portrait of the hapless author and his faithless lover during their trip abroad. It also contains a highly relevant short story by Suslova, "The Stranger and Her Lover," and a number of Dostoevsky's letters.

Fyodor Dostoevsky, *A Writer's Diary*, translated by Kenneth Lantz (Northwestern University Press, 1997). A vast hodgepodge consisting of more than a thousand pages. Seldom has a great writer given such an astonishing insight into how he works, and how his mind works—his insights and his psychology, his unbuttoned comments on life and literature. This is Dostoevsky in the raw, as distinct from speaking through one of his characters.

Joseph Frank, *Dostoevsky*. This is the comprehensive, definitive biography. Few lives and works could be subjected to such lengthy and exhaustive treatment without testing the reader's endurance beyond limits. Admittedly there are a few stretches of tedium, but these are more than outweighed by pages filled with fascinating detail.

Volume 1: *The Seeds of Revolt, 1821–1849* (Princeton University Press, 1986)

Volume 2: *The Years of Ordeal, 1850–1859* (Princeton University Press, 1984)

Volume 3: *The Stir of Liberation, 1860–1865* (Robson Books, 1987)

Volume 4: *The Miraculous Years, 1865–1871* (Princeton University Press, 1996)

Volume 5: *The Mantle of the Prophet, 1871–1881* (Princeton University Press, 2003)

RECOMMENDED READING

Leonid Grossman, *Dostoevsky* (Allen Lane, 1974). A comprehensive biography from the Russian point of view, only partly hampered by the fact that it was written while Russia was still under communism, and thus the authorities regarded Dostoevsky as something of a "dangerous" figure. Offers many insights that could have come from no other source.

Konstantin Mochulsky, *Dostoevsky: His Life and Work* (Princeton University Press, 1967). Criticism rather than biography. Mochulsky is generally regarded as the finest critic of Dostoevsky's work. This book was originally written in Russian and contains many social and philosophical insights into the greater and lesser novels.

Vladimir Nabokov, *Lectures on Russian Literature* (Harcourt Brace Jovanovich, 1981). An amusing and civilized alternative view of Dostoevsky by the great twentieth-century Russian writer, whose grand-uncle was Dostoevsky's jailer in the Peter and Paul Fortress. Judging from this, his grand-nephew would not have let him out.

Richard Peace, *Dostoevsky: An Examination of the Major Novels* (Cambridge University Press, 1971). A thoroughgoing and incisive critique of Dostoevsky's great masterpieces, sketching both his literary development and the processes of his thought and ideas from early skepticism to later religious fanaticism.

Index